HTML

Hyper Text Markup Language

Introduction

This book is a basic primer and introduction to html programming and utilization on the internet or for your intranet at home or business.

The subject is very extensive and this book will attempt to cover all of the various avenues within html, although because of the nature of programming and its expansion and growth during the course of time, you will find that it will be more limited to the basics. We will cover html from 1.0 to 5 (current).

Thanks to the internet we have a large social environment that we as the consumer and casual user can do more than be the average user and can also do light to moderate programming and develop our own web sites and intranets for our personal or business use.

Html is used to make your web pages and even an entire website with limited additions needed.

You no longer have to have a programming degree or understanding the extensive knowledge of programming in order to make a simple web page and with little effort you will be able to create and develop your own website with just this simple introduction to html, the hyper text markup language.

Introduction : Hyper Text Markup Language

Chapter 1 – Basics

HTML stands for Hyper Text Markup Language and was first introduced in 1991. The language is comprised of document tags that represent different content within the HTML document.

A basic HTML document is comprised of the heading, the head, the title, the body and the end tags. You can make an HTML document with an HTML editor or a text editor. Save you pages as page.html to save as an HTML document.

```
<!doctype html> html 5 (2014)
<html> describes the html document
<head> information on the document
<title>Page title</title>
<body> begins the body that is visible
<h1>Heading 1 font size large</h1>
<p>stands for paragraph</p>
</body> ends the body
</html> ends the document
```

The tags of the document are always in pairs with an opening tag that is the beginning and an end tag or closing tag, utilizing an forward slash for the end tag. Only the body section is visible within a browser.

All elements within the document can have attributes and provide additional information about the element such as the language element for your document.

<html lang="en-US"> that stands for english language
<p title="paragraph title"> will indicate the title moused over
A hyperlink can be defined with the <a> tag and end tag </a>
href is the attribute used to define the hyperlink.
<a href="http://www.myvegaslife.com">Nanosoft</a>

Your hyperlink is surrounded by quotes with the web address positioned in between the quotes. No quotes are needed for html5.

You can imput images with the <img> tag. Remember to end all tags, </img>. The size can be determined by using src and utilizing width and height definitions.

<img src="picture.jpg" alt="website.com" width="104" height="80">

The alt attribute is utilized by web page readers and can be read by listeners to the webpage, mainly for the blind. Global attributes can be seen at www.w3schools.com.

Chapter 2 – Headings

Headings are important due to search engines using them to index the content of your web page. Utilizing <h1> as the main and larger heading and so forth as <h2> , <h3> etc.

A horizontal line can be input with the <hr> tag and used to seperate content.

The <head> element tag is used for supplying metadata within your document. This is important for search engines to categorize your document and the data is invisible with the tags.

To start a paragraph you use the <p> </p> elements and you can insert a line break within the paragraph with the <br> element. <pre> is used for preformated text.

Chapter 3 – CSS

Cascading style sheets is added to your document as a seperate file with, <link rel="stylesheet" href="styles.css"> and is placed within the <head> elements </head>. This will call an external document page that is made up of the styles for your document.

You can use inline style such as <h1 style="color:blue;">a Blue heading</h1> Don't forget to put the end tags of all your tags and elements. Or you can use internal css within the <head> tags such as:

```
<style>
body {background-color: blue;}
h1 {color: blue}
p   {color: green}
</style>
```

Chapter 4 – Text

All text for your document that is visible will between the <body> and </body> tags. You can make your text <b> bold and you can make your text <strong> with end tags </b></strong>.

<b>**bold**</b>

You can utilize italics with <i> and emphasis on text with <em> Some more text attributes are.

<i>*italics*</i>

<em>emphasis</em>

<mark>marked text</mark>

<small>small text</small>

<del>deleted text</del>

_{subscript}

^{superscript}

<q>quotes</q>

<cite>cited text</cite>

<address>address text</address>

You can also reverse the direction of your text with <bdo> as in <bdo dir="rtl">changing text from right to left</bdo>

Chapter 5 – Classes

The class attribute defined as <div></div> allows you to define elements with the same name.

```
<style>
div.names {
        color: white;
        margin: 20px 0 20px 0;
        padding: 20px;
}
</style>
</head>
<body>
<div class="names">
</div>
```

Defining the classes within the style element tag means that they are invisible to the rest of the document and is utilizing the internal style editing. <span class="names">names</span> following the <body> tag allows you to use the inline method of classes.

```html
<!DOCTYPE html>
<html>
<head>
<style>
span.names {
    font-size: 120%;
    color: blue;
}
</style>
</head>
<body>
<h1>This span<span class="names">is important</span>
</h1>
</body>
</html>
```

Chapter 6 – Lists

An unordered and an ordered lists are used often in websites for listing items among other things in a data list. An unordered list is indicated by <ul> </ul> followed by the list item <li> </li>.

You can specify the style of the listed item by bullet, circle, square with the inline of <ul style="list-style-type:disc"> replacing disc with circle or square or disc or none.

<ul style="list-style-type:disc">

    <li>milk</li>

    <li>sugar</li>

</ul>

An ordered list starts with the <ol> tag and the list items are the same for either type of list with <li> The ordered list can be defined with the type element marker for type="1" for numbers type="A" uppercase numbers, type="a" lowercase numbers, type="I" for uppercase roman numbers and type="i" for lowercase roman numbers.

```html
<ol type="1">
        <li>coffee</li>
        <li>water</li>
</ol>
```

You can also use a description lists describing each term. Use the <dl> tag to define the list, the <dt> defines the term and the <dd> tag describes each term.

```html
<dl>
        <dt>Coffee</dt>
        <dd>-black hot drink</dd>
        <dt>Milk</dt>
        <dd>-cold drink</dd>
</dl>
```

A nested list is a common element to use and is indicated by either ordered or unordered list items.

```
<ul>
    <li>tea</li>
    <li>black tea</li>
    <li>green tea</li>
</ul>
```

Chapter 7 – Entities

Character entities are necessary when you are dealing with any type of character encoding that represents reserved characters such as < or > for html, but are also used for less than or more than in various fields of study such as mathematics. You can either use an entity name or entity number: &entity_name; or &entity_number; Some browsers don't support names.

Adding a space to your characters you would use   adding a copyright mark you would use either &copy or &#169 for the browsers that don't support names.

Although you won't utilize the entity name spaces on a regular basis, they are good to know or just be aware of that you can find them online in case the need arises when you are writing a scientific article or other similar type of document.

Chapter 8 – Responsive

Respsonsive web design is used for your document when you need it to be seen in various devices such as desktops, tablets or phones. You utilize this by including CSS and HTML in order to resize, enlarge or hide content so that it is viewable on any type of screen.

Inputing the style between your <head> tags you would have for example.

```
<head>
<style>
.list {
        float: left;
        margin: 5px;
        padding:15px;
        max-width: 300px;
        height:  300px;
        border: 1px solid black;
}
```

```html
</style>
</head>
<body>
<h1> Responsive demo</h1>
<div class="list">
```

Chapter 9 – XHTML

XHTML is written as XML. It stands for extensible hyper text markup language and is more strict than HTML. It is supported by all major browers. XML must be well formed and we won't cover it here, but you can find many articles online to further your study on XML. XHTML combines the strengths of XML and HTML.

Chapter 10 – Forms

HTML form elements are used to collect data from the user and is defined within the tags <form> and </form>. They are a type of input element, but unlike checkboxes, radio butotons, submit buttons or other input elements.

The input element is used within the form element as input from the user; <input type="text"> within the text field.

```
<form>
 First name: <br>
<input type="text" name="firstname"<br>
Last name: <br>
<input type="text" name="lastname"<br>
</form>
```

A radio button is indicated by the radio button.

```
<input type="radio" name="type" value="value" checked>
```

The submit button defines the button used for submitting within the form to a form-handler specified in the form's action attribute.

```
<form action="action.php" method="get">
First name: <br>
    <input type="text" name="firstname"
value="value"><br>
Last name: <br>
    <input type="text" name="lastname"
value="value"<br><br>
    <input type="submit" value="Submit">
</form>
```

The method specifieds the type of http method ; either GET or POST that is to be used when submitting the forms. Get is used when the submission is without sensitive information and the Post is used when there is sensitive information that is being submitted.

Fieldset <fieldset> element is used to group elements of related data in a form and the <legend> element is used to define the caption for the fieldset element.

Chapter 11 – Graphics

The canvas element is used to draw graphics but must be accompanied by scripting to create the graphic. There are a few methods available to draw a graphic.

Your browser must be able to support this HTML element. There is an id attribute defined by in the script and a width and height attribute to define the size of the graphic on the canvas.

```
<canvas id="myCanvas" width="200" height="100"></canvas>
```

You can add a border with the style attribute:

```
<canvas id="myCanvas" width="200" height="100" style="border:1px solid #222222;"></canvas>
```

Javascript is most widely used to draw the graphic on your canvas. Here is an example of text.

```
Var c = document.getElementById("myCanvas");

var ctx = c.getContext("2d");

ctx.font = "30px Arial";
```

```
ctx.fillText("Hello World", 10,50);
```

SVG stands for Scalable Vector Graphics and is only used from HTML5, it is used to define graphics for the web. <svg> is used as the element tag for the graphics.

A circle with SVG

```
<svg width="100" height="100">
<circle cx="50" cy="50" r="40"
stroke="blue" stroke-width="4"
fill="green" />
</svg>
```

Chapter 12 – Media

Multimedia video is only available as of HTML 5 and you will need to use mp4 to be available on all platforms (browsers).

Your video content will be shown in a rectangle defined by its height and width within the <video> element.

```
<video width="320" height="240" controls>
<source src="movie.mp4 type="video/mpt4">
<source src="movie.ogg type="video/ogg">
Your browser doesn't support video
</video>
```

Audio is another element that is only available as of HTML5.

```
<audio controls>
<source src="audio.mp3" type="audio/mpeg">
Your browser doesn't support audio
</audio>
```

Chapter 13 – API's

API stands for application programming interface. It is a set of routines and protocols for building your software and wedsites.

Geolocation of HTML is used to get your geographical location of yourself or a user on the internet. This feature can be turned on or off in your browsers settings.

To get a person's position you would used the method for HTML5 and up; getCurrentPosition() and is run in a script or function like Javascript.

Another API is to make element's draggable so you can drop and drag your object by the attribute <img draggable="true">

Application cache is available now and makes your web service available to users while they are offline. It is rather extensive and beyond the basics of HTML, so it will be only a mention in this book.

References

http://www.w3schools.com
http://www.w3.org